Painting and Sculpture

BARRON'S

2

A world of colors

We have wonderful colors in our heads. Some are light and happy, while others are dark and sad. Which ones do you like best? Oscar likes green, but not spinach green; rather lettuce green, which is lighter.

There are many, many shades of green. And brown, and orange, and blue … Which do you think Martha likes the most? How about you?

It's shaped like a ..

Have you ever played at guessing the shapes of the clouds? Wherever you look, you can see a thousand and one different shapes, and the same thing happens with trees. Martha has been drawing all the trees she saw in her walk through the woods. Did you notice how different they look one from the other?

Some trees are tall and thin, like giraffes. Others are short and thick, like a hippopotamus. Which trees do you know? Draw them.

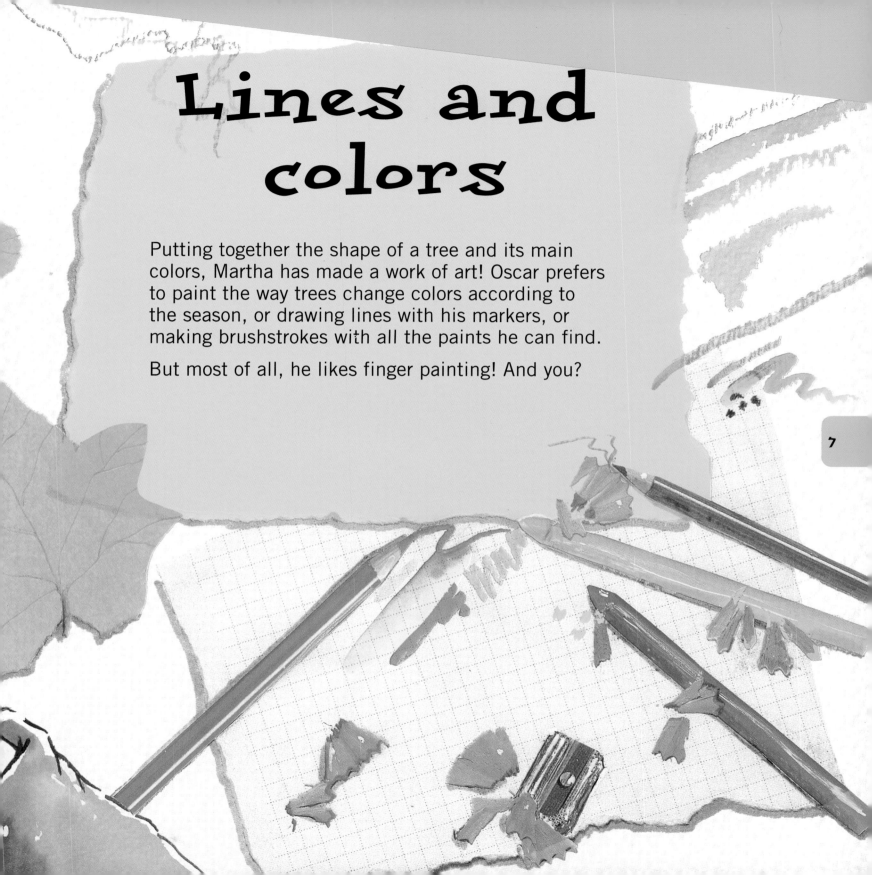

Lines and colors

Putting together the shape of a tree and its main colors, Martha has made a work of art! Oscar prefers to paint the way trees change colors according to the season, or drawing lines with his markers, or making brushstrokes with all the paints he can find.

But most of all, he likes finger painting! And you?

What color is it?

What color is heat? Blue, gray, and purple? Or yellow, orange, and red? Oscar and Martha have discovered there are colors that give a feeling of warmth and others of cold. They know because they painted the same landscape. Martha used cool colors and Oscar used warm ones.

Can you guess which is which? At the end of the book you can find extra help.

In the dark

At
night there are stars
in the sky; sometimes you
see the moon, and you can see
lampposts in the street and lights in
the windows of houses and buildings.
To paint the night you could use some
dark-colored cardboard, such as violet,
black, or navy blue. Watching in the
darkness for a while, you will discover
many new colors.

To paint the moonlight, starlight, or the
light from lampposts you can use
yellow, sky blue, purple, aluminum
foil, and cellophane in
different colors.

Lights and shadows

Oscar pulls the venetian blinds completely shut and then reopens them, but just a little, and asks Martha what she sees in the room. "The same as always," answers Martha, "only colors look darker; they are not as bright as in broad daylight." Yes! Light changes the color of things.

Strange, isn't it? Well, look at the sky. The light coming from the sun can be blue, lilac, light gray, dark gray, pink, red, black … light is magic!

Far . . . near!

What is farthest away in the drawing? And the closest object you can see? Which things are neither far nor near? You can tell at first glance, of course.

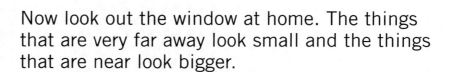

Now look out the window at home. The things that are very far away look small and the things that are near look bigger.

Get some paper and try drawing a landscape with things that are far away and others that are near. You are now an artist!

Jump, turn, wave

Martha and Oscar would like to draw people moving, but they don't know how to do it. They try drawing a boy with his leg up and his arms held over his head: It looks like he is jumping! To practice a little, how about cutting photos out of a magazine, gluing them on a piece of paper, and drawing alongside just the head, arms, and legs?

Sometimes people sit or move in such a way that it seems impossible to draw them!

Let's look for treasure

As you already know, no paints are needed to make pictures. You can make a picture just by gluing pieces of cloth, cotton, newspapers, or any other material to a piece of cardboard. Can you imagine the sea and a sandy beach on a sunny day? You can take pieces of blue cloth with shiny pieces of aluminum foil and make a yellow sky!

If you look around, you can see many objects that will help you describe what you see.

Touch, touch

Pictures are great but they don't let us see what is behind them. Sculptures, however, are different; you can look at them from all around—from the top, from the bottom, from the sides, sometimes you can even look through them. And if you touch them, you can feel if they are smooth or rough.

Touch can be very important in a sculpture!

Imagine

You can use clay, mud, or wet sand to make small sculptures. When you are in the country or at the beach you can create castles, cities, bridges, roads, and mountains. Or maybe you prefer making monsters and weird things with wet sand. Your sculpture can be as different as you want!

But at home there isn't as much room. And your parents will probably not be very happy if you play with mud inside the house! So ask permission before you begin.

24

Boxes, cardboard, and small items

Martha glues together some boxes, and then cuts out pieces of green and yellow cardboard. What is on her mind? Oscar starts to paint shells and pebbles he picked at the beach and, along with pieces of white and brown cloth, attaches them to the cardboard. Can you guess what they are trying to do? A big sculpture!

You can also use various items and materials you have at home and try making large shapes.

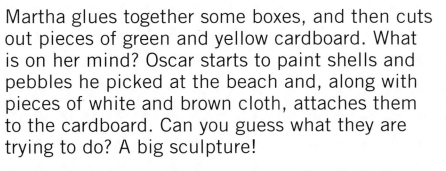

Visiting the museum

The best part of a visit to the museum is finding a picture or a sculpture you especially like and looking at it very carefully. What do you like about that sculpture? Its colors? Its lines? Do you think the picture is a happy one or a sad one? What does the picture represent?

How about the statues you may see in the street? Is there one you like best?

28

What can you explain?

Through art we can explain invisible things; for example, what we feel, what we think, or how we imagine people and things to be. Even in the caves where primitive people lived there are paintings that show how they felt.

The best part of all is that you can have lots of fun painting, making cutouts, pasting, and so forth. That's the way to become an artist!

 A VERY THIN GENTLEMAN

What are the parts of the body? The head, the trunk, and the limbs. With wire that bends easily you can make the figure of a person like the one in the illustration. To make it stand up, just stick it in a base of clay. The best part of this sculpture is that you can make it change its posture every day.

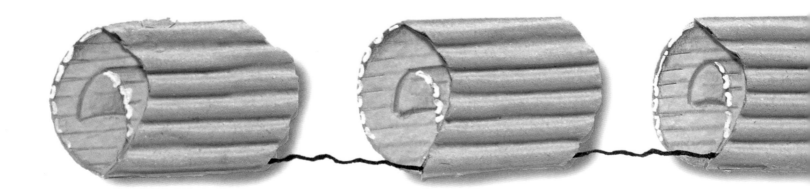

WHAT IF WE DRESS HIM UP?

In a bowl mix some white glue with water (a spoonful of white glue for each spoonful of water). Then tear up newspaper strips and coat them with the glue you have mixed. Now you can dress your figure with the strips of newspaper. Once it is completely dry you can paint it and decorate it as you like. There is only one catch: Now it won't be able to move!

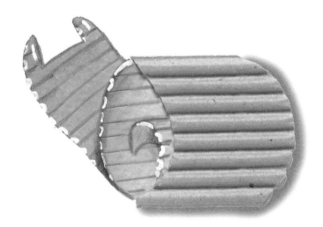

SNAKE

With a piece of corrugated cardboard you will be able to make a snake like this one. All you need is some cardboard and thread to tie all the sections together. How about making a snail?

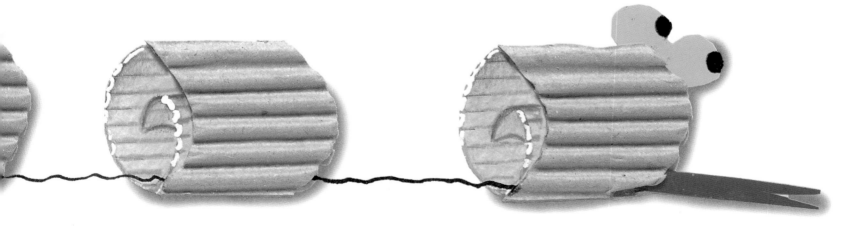

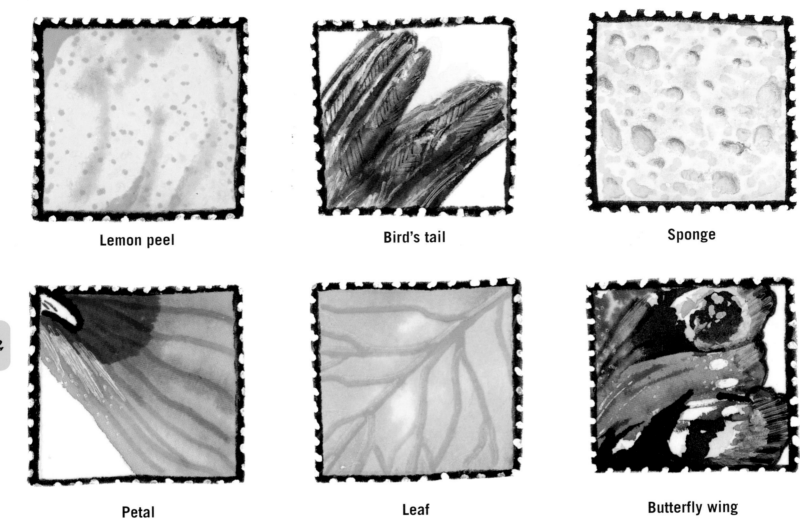

Lemon peel

Bird's tail

Sponge

Petal

Leaf

Butterfly wing

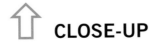

⇧ CLOSE-UP

Did you notice that a close-up look at something makes you discover new details
about it? Look at your skin very closely; can you see tiny holes? Now look at a
leaf from a plant. Could you paint just one part of the leaf? How about drawing
the wings of a butterfly?

32

DIRTY FINGERS

With your fingers wet with paint you can draw a fish swimming in the river, a hen with all her little chicks, and a thousand other things. This is more fun if you use a big piece of paper. Your parents can give you a hand. And you can also paint with your feet!

LOOKING AT A PICTURE

Get a photograph of a painting; you can find one in a magazine, an encyclopedia, or an art book. Look at the picture, alone or in a group of people, and say whether or not there are figures in it, what they are, where the painting was made, under what conditions (weather, day, night, cold, and so on), and how you feel when you look at it. Here are some ideas, but there are many more.

Feelings: Sadness, happiness, anger, joy, envy, mystery, anguish, terror, loneliness.

Figures: Woman, man, child, old man, turtle, dove, ghost, monster, snail, fireman, fish, gorilla.

Places: Sea, mountain, country, village, city, coast, desert, clouds, sky, cave, house, factory, church, road.

Weather and time: Sunny, overcast, rain, noon, afternoon, storm, cold, hot, windy, summer, early.

Does the photo or the painting represent something real, or rather a feeling? Do you like the picture you chose?

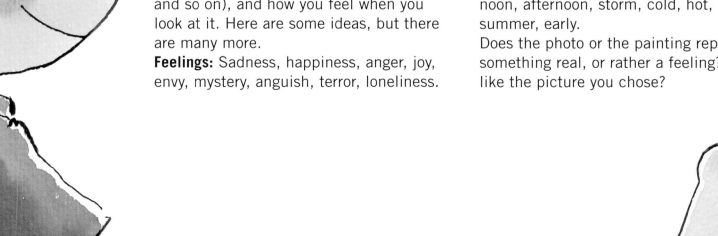

A WORLD OF COLORS

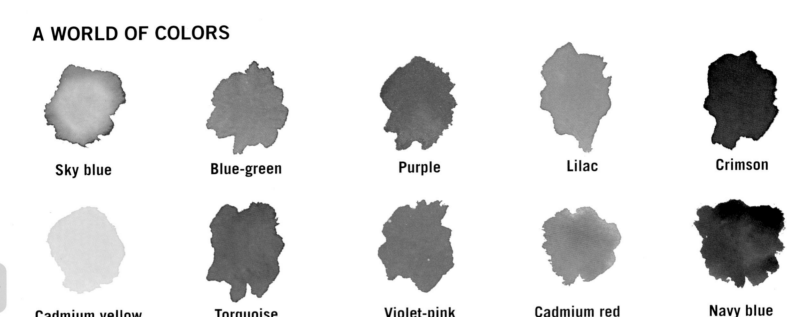

Sky blue   Blue-green   Purple   Lilac   Crimson

Cadmium yellow   Torquoise   Violet-pink   Cadmium red   Navy blue

WARM AND COOL COLORS

Some warm colors . . .

And some cool colors

A FEW INTERESTING FACTS

You can make something that is real or imaginary. You can also paint, draw, or make sculptures that do not have any meaning, just to have fun and to find out what happens while you are making it. You can start trying with:

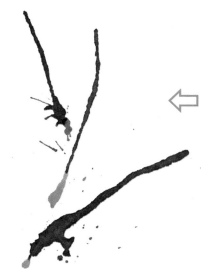

Drinking straw: Get some paint that is not too thick inside the straw and blow. Don't drink the paint.

A roller: You can make wide and long strokes of paint.

A potato: Ask an adult to cut out a figure from a potato and you will have a perfect stamp pad.

An eraser: If you color with a pencil lightly, you can then make white lines erasing part of the drawing.

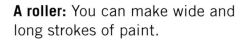

Yogurt container: Make a tiny hole on the bottom, so the paint you put inside will leak drop by drop onto a paper.

Salt: Glued to the paper it can look like dew. Aluminum foil and cellophane provide shine. There are many things you can use to play artist!

A sponge: Wet the sponge in paint and apply it lightly over the paper to fill big spaces. Or press it harder if you wish.

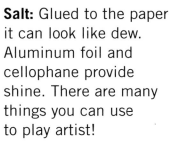

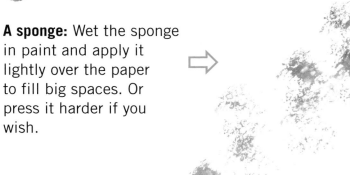

© Copyright Gemser Publications, S.L., 2004.
C/Castell, 38; Teià (08329) Barcelona, Spain (World Rights)
Tel: 93 540 13 53
E-mail: info@mercedesros.com
Author: Núria Roca
Illustrator: Rosa Maria Curto

First edition for the United States and Canada (exclusive
rights), and the rest of the world (non-exclusive rights)
published in 2004 by Barron's Educational Series, Inc.

Address all inquiries to:
Barron's Educational Series, Inc.
250 Wireless Boulevard
Hauppauge, New York 11788
http://www.barronseduc.com

International Standard Book Number 0-7641-2700-4
Library of Congress Catalog Card Number 2003108239

Printed in Spain
9 8 7 6 5 4 3 2 1